love is...

Kim Casali

**with an introduction by
Stefano Casali**

HARRY N. ABRAMS, INC., PUBLISHERS

love is...

love

is...

Introduction

By Stefano Casali

The images collected in this book are loved by many people—but more so by me. They hold an extra-special place in my heart because the boy and girl depicted first represented my parents, Kim and Roberto Casali. Symbols of anyone in love, these two characters are the duo that millions have come to know through the worldwide phenomenon that is *Love Is…*

The seeds for *Love Is…* were planted in the 1960s, when my mother, then known as Kim Grove, met my father, Roberto Casali, at a ski club party in Los Angeles. At the time, my mother was working as a secretary at a cosmetics company, and my father was working as an engineer. There was instant chemistry, and the two of them began dating. Since my mother was shy about expressing her feelings for my father verbally, she put her artistic streak to work and crafted love notes to him that included the now famous characters. The first drawing she made was on a postcard she sent to him from the Mammoth ski resort. She signed the postcard with a little caricature of herself, a caricature so tiny, there was no room for clothes! This was the very first image of the girl we're familiar with today. As time went on, she made more such notes, leaving them in places he'd be sure to find them—under his pillow, in the glove compartment of his car, in his jacket pocket, and in his sock drawer. According to my father, she left drawings for him everywhere! Whenever they were apart, she would send them to him, or he'd find she'd tucked them into the pockets of the shirts he'd brought with him. It wasn't until their wedding day in 1971 that he revealed to her that he'd saved every one she'd ever made for him.

In 1969, my father showed the drawings to a contact of his in the syndication business, who agreed they'd be perfect for syndication. Initially, my mother was not keen on making her drawings public. Not only did she feel they were private doodles, she was worried that she had never properly learned to draw. Finally, after much convincing, on January 5, 1970, the first *Love Is…* cartoon appeared in the *Los Angeles Times*, where it's appeared daily ever since.

Now distributed by Tribune Media Services, the cartoon continues to appear daily in over 100 newspapers worldwide. There are now over 9,000 original panels that have been translated into a multitude of languages. The ones collected in this book are some of my favorites and include the first drawing ever published.

In memory of my parents, it is my dream to maintain

the wonderful legacy that my mother left behind. I'm very proud of the happiness that her work has brought to people all over the world. While my parents are no longer alive, their spirit lives on in these little cartoons.

Love Is... something that starts with two people, is big enough to include other people and the world around us, is a celebration that makes every day a special day, and at its core is really all about two hearts beating as one. I hope that you will turn to *Love Is...* whenever you need a little love in your life.

Right: The first drawing, published on January 5, 1970, in the *Los Angeles Times*

love is...

...not picking the most expensive dish on the menu

love is...

...two people together

love is...

...starting today

love is...

...what surrounds you

love is...

...something that can't be
swept away

love is...

...more than just a formula

...making the right decision

...what changes everything

...radiating an inner warmth

love is...

...the key to happiness

love is...

...the best thing in your life

...clicking

love is...

...like music to your ears

...sharing your problems

love is...

...lending him a helping hand

love is...

...holding out a hand in friendship

love is...

...a new dimension

love is...

...staring your future
in the face

love is...

...not looking back

love is...

...fulfilling when it's natural

love is...

...someone to hold on to

love is...

...getting into the swing
of things

love is...

...a powerful force

love is...

ZAP!

...like a bolt of lightning

love is...

...a miracle

love is...

...being no farther apart than a couch

love is...

...following your heart

love is...

...the shortest route between
two hearts

love is...

...a mountain of kisses

love is...

...the thought that counts

love is...

...like a magic carpet ride

love is...

...guessing into the future,
together

love is...

...always first

love is...

...being swept up in emotion

love is...

...branching out

love is...

...going into orbit

love is...

...at the heart of a relationship

love is...

...a symphony for two players

love is...

...all around you

love is...

...what brightens your day

love is...

...a firm foundation

love is...

...pulling together

love is...

...not maybe—but for real

love is...

...an inspiration

love is...

...a power

love is...

...having a best friend

love is...

...at your fingertips

love is...

...a close encounter of the
best kind

love is...

...chasing rainbows together

love is...

...pedaling the same line

love is...

...admiring the view

love is...

...the journey of a lifetime

...what makes your day

love is...

...driving the blues away

love is...

...a smash hit

love is...

...being generous with
your affection

love is...

...not bottling up your dreams

love is...

...enigmatic

...steadfast in an unpredictable world

love is...

...wine and roses

love is...

...being "romantics"

...when he's your
Prince Charming

love is...

...shared enthusiasms

...something you can't keep a
secret any longer

love is...

...a toast to each other

love is...

...showering her with kisses

love is...

...tears of joy

love is...

...that winning feeling

...the sweetest recipe

love is...

...being in the right place at the right time

love is...

...being there when all seems lost

love is...

...an anchor in a storm

love is...

...in the air

love is...

...a ricksha ride together

love is...

...unforgettable you

love is...

...the little things

love is...

...making each day special

love is...

...adding a little "fizz"

...dancing the last waltz
together

love is...

...washing her car and
polishing it for her

love is...

...sharing the bathroom mirror

love is...

...giving her a tow and asking for her phone number

love is...

...not taking your cell
phone to dinner

110

...wearing matching T-shirts

...watching television in bed

love is...

**...keeping him company
at the laundromat**

love is...

...our cup of tea

love is...

...finding a rose on
your pillow

love is...

**...not buying him the tie of
your choice**

love is...

...taking turns at cooking

love is...

...that special name
he calls you

love is...

...a bottle of champagne when it's not a celebration

love is...

...cheering her up when she's got the "blahs"

love is...

...paint-stained hands

love is...

...giving him homemade
blueberry pie

love is...

...getting up late on Saturday morning

love is...

...meeting under that old oak tree

love is...

...letting her choose the
new car

love is...

...letting her have the first bite

love is...

...a perfect blend

love is...

...a kiss before breakfast

love is...

...a large phone bill

love is...

Kim

...when a day together seems to pass in minutes

love is...

...treating him to a
bubble bath

...going out on the
town together

love is...

...two theater tickets

love is...

...emptying the garbage
without being asked

...taking time off to have fun

love is...

...helping her find her
glasses again

love is...

...supper by candlelight

love is...

Kim

...a turkey sandwich

love is...

...a long good-bye

love is...

...an evening stroll together

love is...

...feeding his parking meter

love is...

...sharing a midnight snack

love is...

...toasting marshmallows
by an open fire

love is...

...cleaning the snow off
her windshield

love is...

...warming his slippers

**...taking brisk evening walks
to keep in shape**

love is...

...sharing the remote control

love is...

...sending her an e-mail love letter

love is...

...finding a love note in
your pocket

love is...

...a sigh

love is...

...someone to help when your
zipper is stuck

love is...

...keeping the phone
handy for his call

love is...

...a daisy chain just for you

love is...

...massaging her toes

...watching old movies together

love is...

...sharing the chocolate
dessert

love is...

...every day,
year round

love is...

...kissing in the new year

love is...

...someone to cuddle on a
winter's walk

love is...

...making the snowman look
like him

love is...

...fastening her ski boots

love is...

...making sure she's well wrapped up

love is...

...belonging to someone
who really loves you

love is...

...saying it with all your heart

love is...

...my gift to you, Valentine

love is...

...seeing the first signs of a thaw

love is...

...waiting in the rain for someone

love is...

...weatherproof

love is...

...what puts the "spring" in
your step

love is...

...a touch of spring fever

love is...

...flowering

love is...

...an "eggspression" of
your affection

love is...

Kim

**...something that needs
tender loving care**

love is...

...a touch of springtime

love is...

...summer madness

love is...

...giving him a sneak preview
of your new bikini

love is...

...someone to rub the sand from your toes

love is...

...sharing your beach
umbrella

love is...

...a time to remember

love is...

...remembering your heritage
on the fourth of July

love is...

...making every day a holiday

love is...

...watching the leaves turn
red and gold

...blowing in the wind

love is...

...not raking up the past like dead leaves

love is...

...the harvest of your
affections

love is...

...being her "fall" guy!

love is...

...going to a Halloween
party with her

love is...

...telling her you'll cook the turkey

love is...

...watching those icicles form

195

love is...

...curling up in front of the
fire in winter

love is...

...chills, thrills...and spills!

love is...

...when he's your snowman

love is...

...walking in a winter
wonderland

...making gingerbread men

love is...

...carol-singing together

love is...

...roasting chestnuts on an
open fire

love is...

...putting the mistletoe up
early

love is...

...hoping for a white Christmas

love is...

...giving his card the best place

love is...

...a little holly and a lot of mistletoe

love is...

...Christmas shopping
for each other

love is...

...filling his stocking

love is...

...a kiss under the mistletoe

love is...

...the best Christmas present

love is...

...making sure no one misses
out at Christmas

kim

love is...

...a traditional Christmas

love is...

Kim

...a Christmas for everyone

love is...

...Christmas at home

love is...

...best when shared

love is...

...kissing away the hurt

love is...

...taking him to your heart

love is...

...a cold, wet nose

love is...

...a game

love is...

...a full tummy

love is...

...showing your affection

love is...

...sharing your quilt

love is...

...one man and his dog

love is...

...playtime

love is...

...saying everything with
a kiss

...dogging her footsteps

love is...

...the way to his heart

love is...

...when you're desperate to make friends with her dog

love is...

...someone to protect you

...never quite what you think

...doing things together

love is...

...letting him share your pillow

love is...

...when three is company

love is...

...all under one roof

love is...

...caring for all God's creatures

love is...

...motherhood

...something precious

love is...

...a bundle of joy

love is...

...a first birthday

love is...

...taking time out to be with the family

love is...

...having unlimited patience

love is...

...being a proud father

love is...

...a bedtime story

love is...

...helping the elderly

love is...

...taking an interest in
her family

love is...

...sharing him with his mother

love is...

...encouraging their search for knowledge

love is...

...watching him proudly
go in to bat

love is...

...someone to take you
fishing

love is...

...letting her sleep late
on Sunday

love is...

...knowing that disciplined
children are nice children

love is...

...what bridges the
generation gap

love is...

...double trouble

love is...

...painting Easter eggs
with the kids

love is...

**...hiking through the bush
with the kids**

love is...

...building a home library

love is...

...teaching your children the importance of good manners

love is...

...taking it lying down

love is...

...when you're all in the
same boat

love is...

...helping her kid brother

love is...

...going camping

love is...

...a warm blanket

love is...

...for everyone

love is....

...a natural high

love is...

...spending your weekend
together

love is...

...a camping vacation

...watching the moon rise together

...singing in the rain

love is...

...landscaping the garden together!

love is...

...teaching him to ride

love is...

...finding your own rainbow

love is...

...writing love letters in
the sand

love is...

...building her a rose arch

love is...

...a family hike

love is...

...going bird-watching
with him

...taking care of our planet

...planting a red rosebush

love is...

...giving her that bonsai she's always wanted

love is...

...planting for the future

love is...

...sitting under a waterfall together

love is...

...camping under the stars

...going for long
country walks together

love is...

...planting an herb garden
for her

love is...

...a home on the range

love is...

...a long weekend—and you

love is...

...turning you green

love is...

...bringing her a plant for her garden

...talking to her plants while
she's away

love is...

...a handful of spring flowers

love is...

...planting her favorite
bulbs for next spring

love is...

...shaving on weekends
during camp-outs

love is...

...using the same bait

love is...

...adjusting her stirrups

love is...

...thinking of the future

love is...

...caring when the going
gets hard

love is...

...being a couple of
wallflowers

309

love is...

...not being a litter bug

love is...

...eating "alfresco"

love is...

...a picnic

love is...

...buying her a bike so you can exercise together

...a halfway house

love is...

...having your heads in
the clouds

love is...

...pulling together

love is...

...watching a sunset on the Nile

...sailing for fun!

love is...

...finding that "silver lining"

love is...

...making ripples

love is...

...believing his story about the
big one that got away

love is...

...watching the moon rise together

love is...

...following him anywhere

love is...

kim

...a splendor of many things

love is...

...the ultimate experience

kiu

love is...

...what it's all about

love is...

...reassuring in an unpredictable world

love is...

...good news

love is...

...marching back into her heart

love is...

...a touching moment

love is...

...the cement that holds us
together

love is...

1 + 1 = ♡

...simple arithmetic

love is...

...coming home safely

love is...

...the key

love is...

...home, where your heart is!

love is...

...a magic that never fades

love is...

...the reason we're together

...being permanently engaged

love is...

...a heart big enough for two

love is...

...knowing you love me

love is...

...what you make it

love is...

...a mutual attraction

love is...

...when the future has never
seemed better

love is...

...when everything's coming up roses

love is...

...communicating

love is...

...what makes a happy home

love is...

...a moment to remember
forever

love is...

...the only language you need

...seeing things "eye to eye "

love is...

...the story of two people

love is...

...within your reach

...intuition

love is...

...a little bit of heaven

love is...

...heaven on earth

love is...

...where nothing can dampen
your spirits

...being his last romance

love is...

...a heart filled with
happiness

love is...

...a big step

love is...

...being surrounded with kisses

love is...

...what all the money in the
world can't buy

love is...

...your good fortune

love is...

...the "zing" in your life

love is...

...the music in your ears

love is...

...what sets you free

373

love is...

...my promise to you

love is...

...the best thing that ever happened to you

love is...

...a store of happy memories

love is...

...something that changes your life

love is...

...making a house a home

love is...

...turning your dream into reality

love is...

...facing the unknown together

love is...

...wanting to make a better world together

love is...

...on the horizon

Designed by Peter Rinzler
Production Manager: Jonathan Lopes

Library of Congress Cataloging-in-Publication Data:

Casali, Kim.
Love is— / Kim Casali ; with an introduction by Stefano Casali.
p. cm.
ISBN 0-8109-4940-7
1. Love—Caricatures and cartoons. 2. American wit and humor, Pictorial. I.
Title.

NC1429.G78A4 2004
741.5'973—dc22
2004006829

Printed and bound in China
10 9 8 7 6 5 4 3

Harry N. Abrams, Inc.
100 Fifth Avenue
New York, NY 10011
www.abramsbooks.com

Abrams is a subsidiary of LA MARTINIÈRE